THEMATIC UNIT
BEARS

Written by Kathy Hofer

Illustrated by Blanca Apodaca, Paula Spence, and Keith Vasconcelles

Teacher Created Materials, Inc.
6421 Industry Way
Westminster, CA 92683
www.teachercreated.com
©1990 Teacher Created Materials, Inc.
Reprinted, 2000
Made in U.S.A.
ISBN 1-55734-267-9

Table of Contents

Introduction

Bears contains a captivating whole language, thematic unit about all kinds of bears, real and fictional. Its 80 exciting pages are filled with a wide variety of lesson ideas and reproducible pages designed for use with early primary children. At its core are two high-quality children's literature selections, *Goldilocks and The Three Bears* and *Good As New*. For each of these books, activities are included which set the stage for reading, encourage the enjoyment of the book, and extend the concepts gained. In addition, the theme is connected to the curriculum with activities in language arts, math, science, social studies, art, music, and life skills (cooking, physical education, etc.) Many of these activities encourage cooperative learning. Suggestions and patterns for bulletin boards and unit management tools are additional time savers for the busy teacher. Furthermore, directions for student-created Big Books and a culminating activity, which allow students to synthesize their knowledge in order to produce products that can be shared beyond the classroom, highlight this very complete teacher resource..

The thematic unit includes:

❏ **literature selections**—summaries of two children's books with related lessons (complete with reproducible pages) that cross the curriculum

❏ **poetry**—suggested selections and lessons enabling students to write and publish their own works

❏ **planning guides**—suggestions for sequencing lessons each day of the unit

❏ **language experience ideas**—daily suggestions as well as activities across the curriculum, including Big Books

❏ **bulletin board ideas**—suggestions and plans for student-created and/or interactive bulletin boards

❏ **homework suggestions**—extending the unit to the child's home

❏ **curriculum connections**—in language arts, math, science, social studies, art, music, and life skills such as cooking, physical education, and career awarness

❏ **group projects**—to foster cooperative learning

❏ **a culminating activity**—which requires students to synthesize their learning to produce a product or engage in an activity that can be shared with others

❏ **a bibliography**—suggesting additional literature and nonfiction books on the theme

---

To keep this valuable resource intact so that it can be used year after year, you may wish to punch holes in the pages and store them in a three-ring binder.

Introduction *(cont.)*

Why Whole Language?

A whole language approach involves children in using all modes of communication: reading, writing, listening, observing, illustrating, experiencing, and doing. Communication skills are interconnected and integrated into lessons that emphasize the whole of language rather than isolating its parts. The lessons revolve around selected literature. Reading is not taught as a separate subject from writing and spelling, for example. A child reads, writes (spelling appropriately for his/her level), speaks, listens, etc. in response to a literature experience introduced by the teacher. In this way, language skills grow naturally, stimulated by involvement and interest in the topic at hand.

Why Thematic Planning

One very useful tool for implementing an integrated whole language program is thematic planning. By choosing a theme with correlating literature selections for a unit of study, a teacher can plan activities throughout the day that lead to a cohesive, in-depth study of the topic. Students will be practicing and applying their skills in meaningful contexts. Consequently, they will tend to learn and retain more. Both teachers and students will be freed from a day that is broken into unrelated segments of isolated drill and practice.

Why Cooperative Learning?

Besides academic skills and content, students need to learn social skills. No longer can this area of development be taken for granted. Students must learn to work cooperatively in groups in order to function well in modern society. Group activities should be a regular part of school life and teachers should consciously include social objectives as well as academic objectives in their planning. For example, a group working together to write a report may need to select a leader. The teacher should make clear to the students and monitor the qualities of good leader-follower group interaction just as he/she would state and monitor the academic goals of the project.

Why Big Books?

An excellent cooperative, whole language activity is the production of Big Books. Groups of students, or the whole class, can apply their language skills, content knowledge, and creativity to produce a Big Book that can become a part of the classroom library to be read and reread. These books make excellent culminating projects for sharing beyond the classroom with parents, librarians, other classes, etc. Big Books can be produced in many ways and this thematic unit book includes directions for at least one method you may choose.

Goldilocks and The Three Bears

Retold by Armand Eisen (or any version)

Summary

This is the story of a little girl, Goldilocks, who goes into the house of the Three Bears when they go for a walk while their porridge cools. She tries their porridge. The biggest bowl is too hot, the medium bowl is too cool, but the little bowl is just right so Goldilocks eats it all up. Next, Goldilocks tries their three chairs and finds one too hard, one too soft and one just right. But, she is too big for the chair, and it breaks. Finally, Goldilocks goes upstairs and tries out the bears' beds. The Father Bear's bed is too hard, the Mother Bear's bed is too soft, but the Little Bear's bed is just right, and Goldilocks falls asleep in the bed. When the bears return, they find Baby Bear's porridge all gone, the broken chair, and then Goldilocks asleep in the bed. When she hears Baby Bear crying, Goldilocks wakes up and quickly runs all the way home.

The outline below is a suggested plan for using the various activities that are presented in this unit. You should adapt these ideas to fit your own classroom situation.

Sample Plan

Day 1

- Share Visiting Bear and his suitcase (page 9)
- List known bears
- Read *Goldilocks and the Three Bears* to the whole class
- Work on story sequence
- Use story props—bears, Goldilocks, bowls, chairs and beds (pages 10-11)
- Bear Puzzle math sheet (page 36)

Day 2

- Review Goldilocks story
- Discuss what Goldilocks did that was not safe; chart answers
- Make safety buttons (pages 7 & 71)
- Make a panel story Big Book (whole class) (page 14)
- Explain centers (page 8)
- Students "read" some of the bear books in the Reading Centers

Day 3

- Make individual scenes for the story (pages 9-13)

- Students retell story using individual story scenes
- Discuss porridge and make enough for the whole class (pages 7 & 60)
- Take a walk in the "woods"
- Write a class language experience story about how the bears felt

Day 4

- Do Getting Ready Activities (page 15)
- Make individual books of *Goldilocks and The Three Bears* (page 15)
- Read books to each other
- Bear Math-sorting, counting, graphing (pages 37-38)

Day 5

- Act out the story using creative dramatics
- Study characters, setting, and problem
- Begin studying real bears (see plan, page 41)

Overview of Activities

SETTING THE STAGE

1. Prepare your classroom for a unit on bears. Assemble the bulletin board. Directions and patterns are on pages 67 to 70. Set up the learning centers and displays described on pages 8 and 9. Send home the letter to parents announcing the start of the unit and requesting materials (page 75).

2. Prepare one set of the story props (pages 10-11). Duplicate, color, laminate, and attach to craft sticks or tongue depressors. (You may wish to enlarge them.)

3. Introduce the unit by having the class meet The Visiting Bear (see page 9). Describe his visits home and the postcard activity. Assign the first visit—lucky child! Be sure to send the note to parents that describes this activity (page 74) with the bear each night.

4. Have children name, while you list on the board, any real and story bears they know. Accept any answers now but make sure false information is corrected before the unit is over; e.g., koalas and pandas are not really bears.

REAL BEARS	STORY BEARS
Polar Grizzly	Winnie-the-Pooh Corduroy The Three Bears Ira's Teddy Bear, Tah Tah

5. Gather the children and show them the cover or first page of *Goldilocks and the Three Bears.* Have them tell you what book it is and how they know. Ask them to tell you who is in the book (characters) and where the story happens (setting). Be sure to discuss whether these bears are real or imaginary—nonfiction or fiction. How can the children tell?

ENJOYING THE BOOK

1. Read *Goldilocks and the Three Bears* aloud to the children.

2. Discuss the order of the events in the story. Let the children know that sequence is another word for order. Pass out the story props, one per child. Reread the story letting the children with the props use them as puppets to enact the story. Let those with Goldilocks and the bears speak the appropriate lines. Pause several times to ask, "What happens next?" or "Which prop will we need next?"

3. Make a Panel Story/Big Book for *Goldilocks and the Three Bears.* Complete directions are on page 14.

4. Review what Goldilocks did in the story. You may want to read another version to the children. (See Bibliography, page 79 for suggestions.) Guide the children to make a list with you of what Goldilocks should not have done.

- *Went into the woods alone*
- *Did not tell where he was going*
- *Went into a stranger's house*
- *Broke a chair*
- *Ate food that could have been bad*
- *Went to sleep in a stranger's bed*

Talk about how these things are not safe. Remind the children that Goldilocks was not a real girl and that the story did not really happen.

Overview of Activities (cont.)

ENJOYING THE BOOK (cont.)

5. Have students make "Be Beary Safe" buttons using the pattern on page 71. These may be used with a button maker or mounted on tagboard with an attached safety pin.

6. Have children make their own scene and props. Directions are on page 9. Patterns for props are on pages 10-13. Then let them take turns telling the story in small groups of 2 to 4 children. Save these to use with the Hear Me-See Me activity described on page 9.

7. Individually, or in small groups, students read and/or look at bear books—fiction and nonfiction—from the Reading Centers (see page 8).

8. Talk about porridge. Let the children know that porridge is another name for hot cereal like oatmeal. Make hot oatmeal (see page 60 for recipe).

9. While the "porridge" is cooling, take the children outside. Talk about what the three bears might have seen during their walk in the woods. Return to the room to sample the "porridge." Draw pictures of the "woods."

10. Write a language experience story as a group about the three bears' feelings during the story.

11. Make individual Three Bears books. Choose one of the options described on page 15. When the books are completed, do the Hear Me-See Me activity described on page 9.

EXTENDING THE BOOK

1. Act out the story using creative dramatics. The students make up their own words as they go along. Keep things moving so everyone has a turn. (Bear Book Cover, page 31, may be used as a mask by attaching strings or pipecleaners to sides or a tongue depressor to bottom. Be sure to cut eyeholes!)

2. Read several stories about bears to the class. Talk about how all stories have:

   characters –   the people or animals that act out the story
   setting –   the place the story took place
   problem –   what happened in the story.

   With the class, write the names of any bear books read to the class and then the title, *Goldilocks and the Three Bears* on the board. Have the class supply the characters, setting and problem for each story.

3. Begin your study of real bears. See pages 41 to 54. Students can decorate a large, folded piece of construction paper as a cover for a folder to collect their real bear papers. Later, these can be stapled into a booklet to be taken home.

Beary Fine Learning Centers

Literature Reading Center

There are lots of books with bears on the market today. Assemble as many as possible at a reading center. Make this area a comfortable place to be by providing pillows, rug, etc. The children could be asked to bring bear books to share with the class. Remind them to be sure that their names are in the books and then set up a special reading table for the children to put the books on when they bring them in. You may even find that enough multiple copies of some of the books come in so that you can borrow them for small group reading.

Science Reading Center

The teacher should also collect books on real bears. Set up a science center to house these books. Children will learn by looking at bear pictures even if they cannot read the books. Near the science center, post a large piece of butcher paper divided into four or more sections (one for each kind of real bear). When the children learn a fact about a certain kind of bear, they can write or dictate that fact onto a paper bear (pattern, page 77) with their name, cut it out and then paste it onto the correct section of the butcher paper.

Art Center

Set up an art center for bears. The children can choose from several different mediums to complete a bear. Have basic bear patterns available for them to trace on their art paper. (See patterns, p. 58) They can then outline the pattern with dark crayon and fill it in with foam packaging pieces, twisted tissue paper balls, or squares of tissue twisted on the end of a pencil and then dipped into white glue. Sponge painting of white tempera paint on brown construction paper also works nicely. After they have completed the Drawing Bears worksheet (p. 56), they can use crayon or chalk to make their own complete bear in the woods, North Pole or other scene.

Writing Center

Students will enjoy having the opportunity to write or dictate their own books about bears to share with the rest of the class. The teacher can have pre-folded books on which the children can put their bear stories (directions on page 15). It's nice to have a basket to put the completed stories in so the children can read them when they finish their work. This also lets the children know where to put their books when they are finished and encourages them to finish one.

Beary Special Activities

The Visiting Bear

You might want to consider buying a special bear for the children to take home for a night. It would be especially fun if you pack a "suitcase" of special things that the bear might like. Tell the children that they may dress the bear or add to the suitcase if they want to. The only rule is that they have to take good care of the bear. They can't leave the bear where it will get hurt by the family dog, etc. They also will need to bring the bear back on time so that the next person can take the bear home. The Bear Record Sheet (page 73) works nicely if you want to post a list so students can see whose turn is next. Give the child whose turn it is a large index card so that he and the bear (with the family's help) can write the class a picture postcard about the visit. Page 74 is a letter to parents describing the visit and postcard activity.

Teddy Bear Display

Suggest that it would be fun for the children to bring their favorite teddy bear to school to share. Prepare a special table(s) with a blanket or quilt to set a teddy bear display on. When you read a story on the rug, you might let the children bring their bears to the rug to listen to the story. And, young children find it enjoyable to read to their bears. (You might wish to let children bring other favorite stuffed animals or toys if they do not have a bear so that no one is left out.)

Making and Using the Story Props

Have children make a set of the story props (pages 10-13). Reproduce patterns onto tagboard. Have children color and cut them out. Attach the characters to tongue depressors or craft sticks so they can be used as puppets. Glue the other props into the cottage rooms (overlap beds) and add background. The cottage may be attached to the lid of a shoe box (it will be longer than the lid). The box with the lid on, placed on its side, will serve as the "stage." The puppets can be stored in the box when not in use. Children should practice using the props to retell the story to one another in small groups. The props are then taken home for the Hear Me—See Me activity described below.

Hear Me — See Me

Have children make their own Three Bears book. Choose one of the options from page 15, depending on the ability of your students. When the books are completed, have students practice reading them to each other. Give out coupons (pattern, page 71) for the students to award to one another. When they think they are ready, children put their books in a basket or box that the teacher has provided. An adult (teacher, parent volunteer, etc.) can then call on the children to read their finished books. Then students take their books, scene, and props home to read and tell to 3-5 significant others (one at a time). Use Hear Me—See Me letter, page 76, to announce this activity to families and solicit their cooperation.

Story Props

* See pages 6 and 9 for suggested uses.

Story Props

* See pages 6 and 9 for suggestions.

Story Props

Bears' Cottage — Part 1   * See page 9 for suggestions.

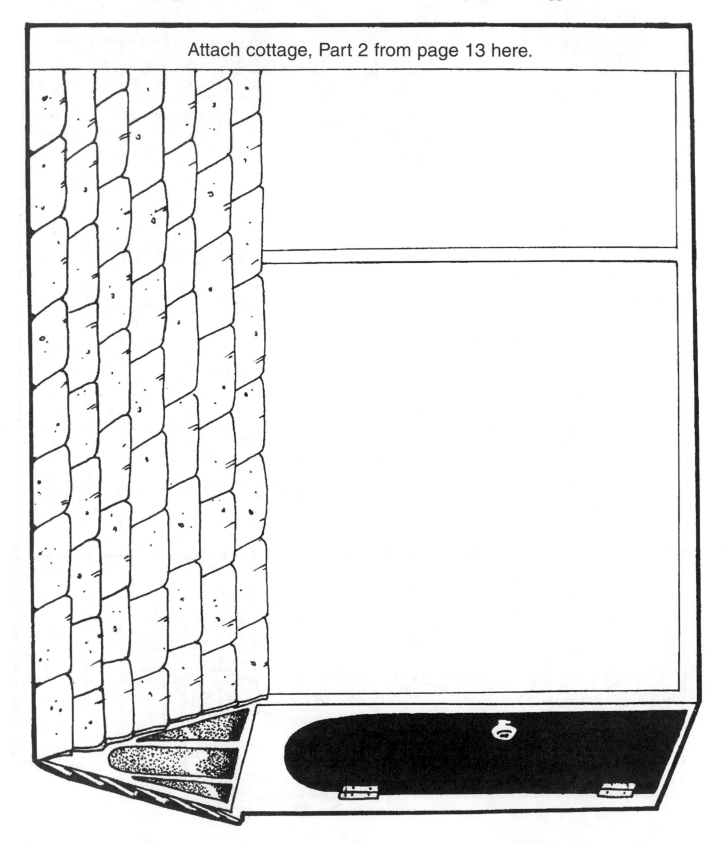

Attach cottage, Part 2 from page 13 here.

Story Props

Bears' Cottage — Part 2
*See page 9 for suggestions.

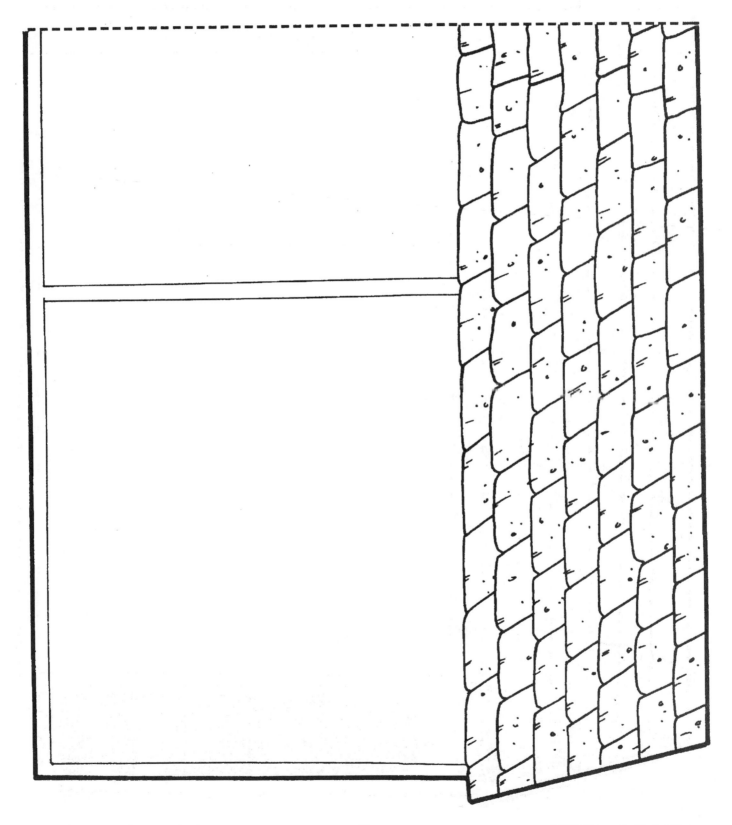

Making a Panel Story/Big Book

1. Cut butcher or white shelf paper into a 12 foot (3.6 meters) length.

2. Accordion fold the paper into eight 18 inch (45 cm) sections. (See diagram.)

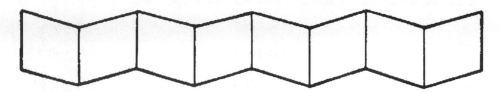

3. Unfold the paper and draw lines on the folds.

4. Post the paper or spread it on the floor so that the children can reach it for drawing and coloring.

5. Print the following sentences on the panels:

   Panel 1:   The bears' porridge was too hot.
   Panel 2:   The bears went for a walk.
   Panel 3:   Goldilocks went into the bears' house.
   Panel 4:   She ate the porridge.
   Panel 5:   She broke the chair.
   Panel 6:   She went to sleep.
   Panel 7:   The bears found Goldilocks.
   Panel 8:   Goldilocks ran home.

   Or, have children help compose the sentences. This is a good activity for checking the concept of sequencing of story events.

6. Let small groups of children draw and color a picture for each page. To avoid crowding, one group should work at a time!

7. Hang the panel story on the wall as a mural and practice it each day for several days until the children are successful at reading it themselves.

8. Take the panel story down and refold it accordion-style. Add title. Staple very close to the left edge. Tape over staples for durability.

  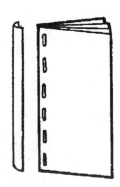 

Make a Three Bears Book

Getting Ready

1. Practice the repetitive vocabulary of *Goldilocks and the Three Bears* with the children. Make word, phrase, and sentence strips for the vocabulary you wish to emphasize.

   the three bears   **too cold**   **too hot**

   Goldilocks   **too hard**   **too soft**

   Somebody's been sleeping in my bed!   **And here she is!**   **just right**

   As the story is read or told, place (or have the children find and place) the strips on the chalk tray, in a chart rack, or on a flannel or magnetic board.

2. Use page 16 to practice or check some of the vocabulary.

3. Choose one of the bookmaking activities below depending on the ability of your students.

Fill-In Books

1. Copy pages 17 to 20 on front and back of paper using photocopy or ditto.

2. Arrange pages in the correct order, paying attention that the tops are all in the same direction.

3. Staple in the middle with a long-armed stapler if one is available. If not available, fold shut and staple close to the folded edge.

4. Rehearse some ways to fill in the blanks developing a Word Bank on the board. Then let students complete their own book.

Folded Books

1. First, fold the paper in half once the long way.

2. Next, unfold and fold twice in the opposite direction.

3. Open the last fold; then cut according to diagram.

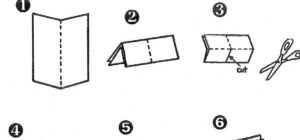

4. Open all the way. Then refold the long way and push out the center.

5. Continue pushing until the center comes together

6. Crease and fold into a little book.

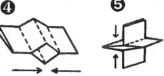

This makes an 8 page blank book to be used for writing and/or illustrating original books.

Shape Books

Use the patterns and directions on pages 31 and 32 to make bear-shaped books in which students can record their original stories and pictures.

Beary Good Words

_____

_ _ _ _ _ _ _ _ _ _ _ _ _ _ _ _ _

too _____

too _ _ _ _ _ _ _ _ _ _ _ _ _

just _____

too _____

_____

too _ _ _ _ _ _ _ _ _ _

_ _ _ _ _ _ _ _ _ _ _ _ _ _ _

Word Box	bears	cold	Goldilocks
	cottage	soft	home
	hot	hard	right

Goldilocks runs

Page 7

_____

_____ .

Fold here

by

_____

retold and illustrated

_____ .

Goldilocks and the Three Bears

The three bears find _____

go

The three _____
for a walk.

18

Father Bear's bed is too _____.

Mother Bear's bed is too _____.

Baby Bear's bed is _____.

So Goldilocks goes to sleep.

Page 5

Fold here

Goldilocks goes into the three bears' _____.

Goldilocks goes into the

Page 2

Father Bear's chair is too _____.

Mother Bear's chair is too _____.

Baby Bear's chair is _____.

But Goldilocks breaks it.

Page 4

Father Bear's porridge is too _____.

Mother Bear's porridge is too _____.

Baby Bear's porridge is _____.

So Goldilocks eats it.

Page 3

Good As New

by Barbara Douglass

Summary

This is the story of how Grady's cousin ruins Grady's teddy bear by dragging it around by the ears, feeding it peanut butter, turning the hose on it, and then burying it in the sand in the back yard. After his cousin leaves, Grandpa promises to fix Grady's bear. Grandpa takes out the stuffing, washes the bear, buys new stuffing and makes it not good as new, but better than new.

The outline below is a suggested plan for using the various activities that are presented in this unit. You should adapt these ideas to fit your own classroom situation.

Sample Plan

Day 1

- Predict from the cover what *Good As New* will be about

- Chart predictions

- Read story to page 3 "To Share or Not" activity (page 22)

- Graph student responses

- Continue study of real bears (see page 41) each day

Day 2

- Review story part from yesterday

- Read story to page 7

- Students illustrate and/or write what happened when K.C. held Grady's bear (page 22)

- Students read panel stories to each other

- Good As New Math (pages 39-40)

Day 3

- Read the rest of the story to the class

- Discuss story :

- "If I Were Grady" activity (page 23)

- Make bear bookmarks

Day 4

- Students make stuffed bears

- Reread whole story to class

- Discuss favorite part and why

- Make and share a class book of favorite parts of the story

Day 5

- Worksheet—Make It Good As New (page 26)

- Good As New Chant Poem (pages 27-28)

- Read other bear stories to the class

- Continue study of real bears

- Plan for Culminating Act

Day 6

- Culminating Activity—Teddy Bears' Picnic

Overview of Activities

SETTING THE STAGE

1. Show the students the cover of *Good As New*. Read the title to them and then give them a chance to predict what the story will be about. Let them know that the bear on the cover is a little boy's favorite teddy bear. Chart the children's predictions and the reasons for their predictions.

2. Ask students if they have ever had to share something that was very special to them even though they didn't want to. Tell them that this story is about what happened when a boy named Grady had to share his special teddy bear with his cousin, K.C.

ENJOYING THE BOOK

1. Read the story through to page 3 where Dad said, "Do you think he might feel better, son, if you just let him hold your bear?"

2. Have students write or tell whether they would let K.C. hold the teddy bear.

3. Make a class graph. **Hint:** Let each child have a piece of sticky notepad on which to write or draw the decision. Then post it on a class graph.

To Share or Not													
Share the bear													
Not share the bear													

4. When y u are ready to begin reading th ned in the first part of the story. Then have them tell their neighbor. Have several children share with the whole class what they heard.

5. Continue reading the story to page 7 where Grady says, "I don't want a new bear. I want this old one fixed the way he was before K.C. came."

6. Give the students a piece of white art paper cut to about 9" x 24". Have them fold the paper two times so that there are four panels to draw on when they open the paper. Ask the children what K.C. did to the bear when he first took him. If they are able, have them write a sentence describing that in the first panel. Continue with each panel until one sentence is written for each. Then have the children illustrate each panel. (Non-writers may make only illustrations.) Note that there are six possible situations for the children to choose from.

7. Children should read their panel stories to at least 5 different people. The child or adult who has heard the story should write his/her name on the back of the panel story. Or, duplicate the tickets (page 71) for students to have signed as they share their panel stories. Post stories around the room.

8. Tell the children that now they are going to hear what Grandpa did about Grady's ruined teddy bear. Reread page 1 so the children are reminded that "Grandpa could fix anything." Then, read through to the end of the story.

Overview of Activities *(cont.)*

ENJOYING THE BOOK *(cont.)*

9. Talk about the following:

- *How did Grady feel when Grandpa got out his pocket knife? Why do you think he felt that way?*
- *When Grandpa took the stuffing out of the bear's stomach, Grady said, "My bear's stomach went flat, the way mine feels when I'm hungry." What did Grady mean by that? Grandpa kept saying, "Never you mind now, Grady." What did Grandpa mean?*
- *When Grandpa started stuffing the bear, Grady thought the "stomach still looked hungry." What did that mean?*
- *After Grandpa finished stuffing the bear, he sewed on the ears. Grady looked at his bear and told his Grandpa, "I thought you could fix anything. But this bear isn't good as new." This made Grandpa feel sad. What did Grady tell his Grandpa after that?*

10. "Now whenever K.C. comes to visit, Grandpa and I grab our hats (and my bear) and slip out the back door, neverminding." What does that mean? Record student answers on board or chart paper. Make a class list of what you would do to avoid trouble if K.C. were your cousin and he was coming to visit. Read the list over by rows, teams, boys, girls, etc. until it has been read many times.

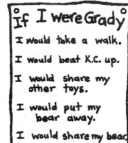

11. Make bear bookmarks (page 71) to encourage bear "reading."

EXTENDING THE BOOK

1. Make teddy bears. Directions and pattern are on pages 24-25. Discuss whether all teddy bears look alike. How could we make them different?

2. Reread the whole story *Good As New* through to the children.

3. Talk about the students' favorite part of the story and why it's their favorite. Have them write and/or illustrate it. These may be done on, or glued to, 9" x 12" construction paper. Remind them all to turn their paper the same way for a class book. As a class decide on a cover.

4. Read the class book together on the rug. Students can read their own page when it comes up.

5. Do "Make It Good As New" worksheet (page 26) as an introduction to the following activity.

6. Create a variation of the Good As New Chant Poem (pages 27-28). Assemble illustrated poems into a class book.

7. Continue your study of real bears (see page 41).

Make Your Own Teddy Bears

1. Duplicate pages 24-25 onto heavy paper or make 6-8 patterns on tagboard for the students to trace onto heavy paper or felt.

2. Decorate bear with crayons or scraps of lace, ribbon, fabric, wallpaper, etc.

3. Staple front and back together or punch holes around the bear and "stitch." Do this by using long shoelaces, yarn with ends dipped in white glue and dried, or yarn with ends wrapped in tape.

Directions continued on next page.

Make Your Own Teddy Bears *(cont.)*

4. Leave space between ears open for stuffing.

5. Stuff with commercial stuffing, batting, cotton balls, or small, wadded pieces of paper.

6. Close opening.

Name_____

Make It Good As New

1. Fix these by drawing their missing parts.   2. Trace the words.

teddy bear

wagon

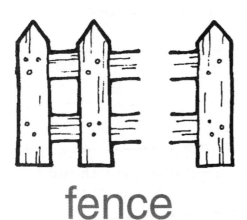

fence

fire engine

sandbox

swing

Creating a Chant Poem

This activity provides a way to practice some of the vocabulary from *Good As New*.

1. Share the following poem with the class after rereading the first page of *Good As New*.

> **Grandpa can fix anything.**
> **He can make it good as new.**
> **He can fix a swing.**
> **He can fix a fire engine.**
> **He can fix a sandbox.**
> **He can fix a bear.**
> **He can make them good as new.**

2. Brainstorm with the children other things Grandpa might be able to fix. Create a Word Bank on chart paper or an overhead projector. Help the children classify their suggestions.

Fix-It Word Bank			
Toys	**In the Yard**	**In the House**	**Vehicles**
bike	fence	dishwasher	car
doll	hose	leaking faucet	motorcycle
truck	sidewalk	plugged drain	bus
			airplane

3. Make a chart of the worksheet on page 28 or display it on the overhead projector. Or, make sentence strips for a pocket chart. Model filling in the blanks using words from the Fix-It Word Bank.

4. Pair students who work well together. Give each pair a copy of page 28 and have them work together to fill in the blanks using the Word Bank or other words they think of. Have them illustrate their poem.

5. Have students share their illustration and poem, with partners chanting aloud in unison.

6. Assemble the poems and illustrations into a book for the class library to be enjoyed throughout the year.

Variations:

1. Change the name of the fixer—Dad, Mom, a mechanic, your name, etc. How does this influence the objects being fixed?

2. Brainstorm words that mean about the same as fix—mend, correct, patch, clean, repair. Substitute them for "fix" in the poem. How does this influence the choice of the fixer and objects to be fixed?

Good As New Chant Poem

Written and illustrated by _____

_____

Grandpa can fix anything.

He can make it good as new.

He can fix _____

He can fix _____

He can fix _____

He can fix _____

He can make them good as new.

28

Bear Poems

A good collection of poems for young children on almost any subject is *Read-Aloud Rhymes for the Very Young*, selected by Jack Prelutsky. The poems referred to below are from this book unless otherwise noted.

A Year in the Life of a Bear

The poem "Wild Beasts" by Evelyn Stein suggests a fun activity for children. Have them make bear "dens" by putting blankets over tables and chairs. Let them imitate the growl and four-footed walk of a bear all around the room. Provide some snacks for the "bears" to munch on before "denning." Fruit, nuts, small crackers to be eaten with honey in a squeeze bottle and/or tuna fish are possibilities. Then have your little bears crawl into their dens for their long winter naps. "Grandpa Bear's Lullaby" by Jane Yolen (in *The Random House Book of Poetry for Children,* selected by Jack Prelutsky, Random House, 1983) is a wonderful poem to use to quiet the excited bears as they role-play the bears' sleep.

Another poem about animals preparing for winter is "In the Summer We Eat" by Zhenya Gray. Since this poem does not mention the word bears, it's a good one to read and then ask the children to tell you what it is about.

Bear Couplets

Use Gail Kredenser's "Polar Bear" poem to stimulate the writing of other two-line rhyming poems about bears. For example:

One kind of bear is called a grizzly.

His fur is brown and kind of frizzly.

Teddy Bears

There are many cute poems that express an owner's love of his/her teddy bear. Two of them are named "My Teddy Bear"—one by Marchette Chute and the other by Margaret Hillert.

And, of course, one cannot ignore the old jump rope rhyme reprinted below. This is a good one to do with actions (with or without a jump rope). You and the children will be able to write and enact many variations.

Teddy Bear, Teddy Bear,	**Teddy Bear, Teddy Bear,**
Go upstairs.	**Touch your toes.**
Teddy Bear, Teddy Bear,	**Teddy Bear, Teddy Bear,**
Say your prayers.	**Touch your nose.**
Teddy Bear, Teddy Bear,	**Teddy Bear, Teddy Bear,**
Turn out the light.	**Turn around.**
Teddy Bear, Teddy Bear,	**Teddy Bear, Teddy Bear,**
Say good night.	**Touch the ground.**

Daily Language Experience Activities

Since whole language encompasses speaking, listening, reading and writing, it is important to include all of these as part of the daily program. These are prompts that can be used for daily language experience activities. During discussion the teacher should record student responses or have students write their own when they are able.

1. If I were a bear, I would...
2. If I were a bear, the first thing I would do after winter would be...
3. Bears have sharp claws to...
4. Bears have fur coats to...
5. If I were Goldilocks, I would...
6. If I were Goldilocks, I would not...
7. If I were walking through the woods and saw a grizzly, I would...
8. The bear was scary because...
9. Smokey the Bear says...
10. One day I lost my teddy bear and...
11. I like my teddy bear because...
12. It makes me feel good to sleep with my teddy because...
13. Once when we were camping I saw a bear and...
14. Bears need heavy fur because...
15. If I wanted to see a real bear, I'd...
16. Bears use their paws to...
17. K.C. was _____ because...
18. It's not safe to make friends with a bear because...
19. The neat thing about Grady's grandpa was...
20. Grady's bear was better than new because...
21. What do bears do for fun?
22. Pretend you are a bear and write about humans.
23. What would you tell your children to do if they ran into a bear in the forest?
24. Describe the perfect teddy bear.
25. If you were a bear, what would you pack for your long winter's hibernation?

If your students are beginning to write on their own, don't forget—Writing is a process that includes:

1. Pre-writing (Get ready to write.)
2. Writing (Try to encourage flow of ideas without perfection getting in the way.)
3. Self-editing (Teach kids to check and correct their own work.)
4. Responding (Have an adult or another child comment on the story.)
5. Re-writing (Make corrections, additions, deletions, etc.)

Bear Shape Book

Reproduce onto construction paper (pink, yellow, brown).

Students add color and personality with crayons.

Students write title and their name as author.

Cut out

Cover

Bear Shape Book *(cont.)*

Use this page to make patterns to trace on lined newsprint or duplicate enough for each child to write their own book.

Bear Word Search

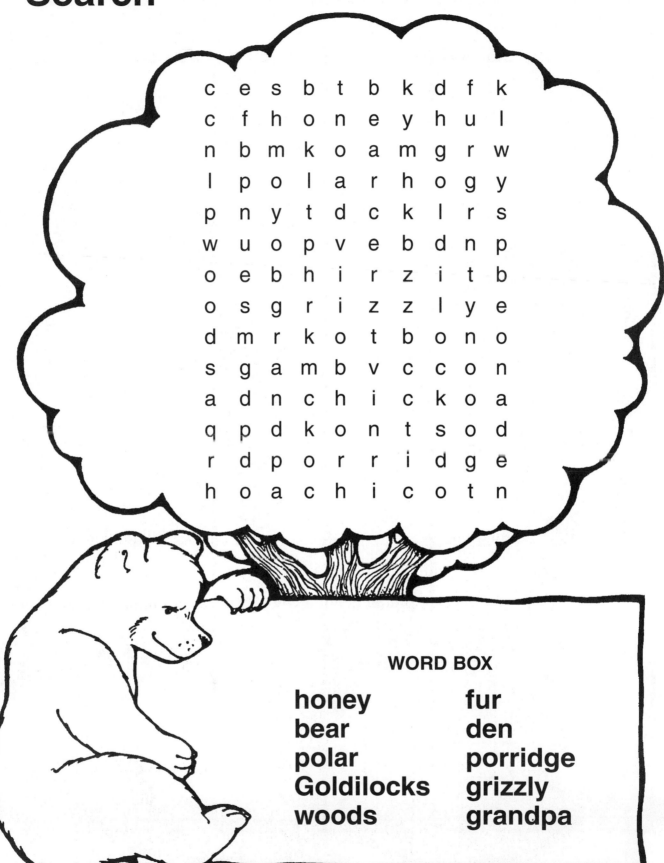

```
c e s b t b k d f k
c f h o n e y h u l
n b m k o a m g r w
l p o l a r h o g y
p n y t d c k l r s
w u o p v e b d n p
o e b h i r z i t b
o s g r i z z l y e
d m r k o t b o n o
s g a m b v c c o n
a d n c h i c k o a
q p d k o n t s o d
r d p o r r i d g e
h o a c h i c o t n
```

WORD BOX

honey	fur
bear	den
polar	porridge
Goldilocks	grizzly
woods	grandpa

Bare Bear

1. Write the correct one.   2. Color.

bear   bare

About The Author and Illustrator

Children need to know that authors are real people. They also need to know that the illustrator is not usually the author, but rather someone who is good at drawing pictures. A good source for this information is the volumes of *Something About the Author* (edited by Anne Commire. Gale Research, Detroit, MI, updated regularly) found in most libraries.

Barbara Douglass is from Elk Grove, California. She has written many books for children. One called *Skateboard Scramble* was made into a film called "A Different Kind of Winning. " As a child she loved books and reading.

Patience Brewster lives in Skaneateles, New York. She went to art school in Philadelphia. Her husband convinced her to try illustrating children's books, and she began when she was expecting her first baby. She uses pencil and paint with ink or watercolor. Among the other books she has illustrated are *I Met a Polar Bear* by S. & P. Boyd (Lothrop, 1983) and *Oh, Brother* by P. Laiken (Little, Brown, 1987). She has two children and had to do her art while taking care of them when they were small.

Divide the children up into groups and have them work together to do the following:

1. Write a letter to Barbara Douglass and tell her how much they enjoyed her book. Ask her why her book was dedicated to her two grandfathers. Were they like Grady's grandfather?

2. Draw pictures with captions to retell *Good As New* for Ms. Douglass.

3. Write a letter to Patience Brewster and tell her how they liked the illustrations in *Good As New*. Find out what other books she has illustrated so that they can look at some of her other illustrations. Find out what she used to make the illustrations.

4. Try making some illustrations like Ms. Brewster did for *Good As New*.

Send Letters to:

Ms. Barbara Douglass
c/o Lothrop Lee Shepard Books
105 Madison Avenue
New York, NY 10016

Ms. Patience Brewster
c/o Lothrop Lee Shepard Books
105 Madison Avenue
New York, NY 10016

Bear Puzzle Math Sheet

Color Code

brown	**5**
yellow	**6**
blue	**7**
red	**8**

1. Add.

2. Write the numeral

3. Color using the color code.

4. Cut, put together, and paste onto a large sheet of white construction paper.

5. Add sky, background, and other bears.

3+3= ___

3+4= ___

1+4= ___

3+2= ___

2+3= ___

4+1= ___

4+4= ___

Sorting and Counting Bears

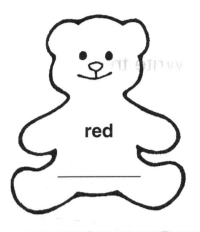
red
_____

1. Sort your Bears
2. Put them in the right box.
3. Count.
4. Write the numeral on the line.
5. Fill in page 36.

yellow
_____

white
_____

orange
_____

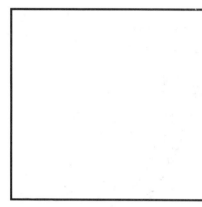
green
_____

Teacher:

Students may work alone or in groups. Teacher must supply paper bears, plastic bear counters (see Bibliography, page 79, for source), or bear-shaped foods (check candy, crackers, cereal, and cookie departments). Change this page and the next to match the product(s) used.

Graphing Bears

1. Color or label each bear to match the bears on the sorting sheet.
2. Fill in one box on the graph for each bear counted.

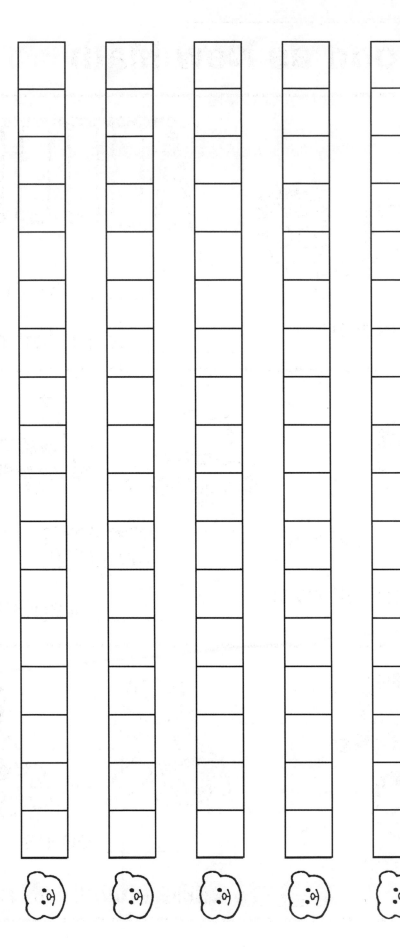

Which color was the greatest? _____

Which color was the least? _____

Which is the total of the red and green bears? _____

What is the total of the orange and yellow bears? _____

Teacher: This page can be enlarged and done together as a class.

Good as New Math

Write the numerals.

 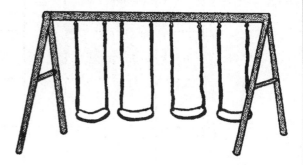

_____ swings

_____ children

_____ swing left over

_____ children

_____ wagon left over

_____ wagons

_____ children

_____ bears

_____ children with no bears

Good as New Math (cont.)

_____ spools of thread

_____ needles   _____ extra needles

_____ children

_____ extra popcorn   _____ boxes of popcorn

Challenge:

_____ ears

_____ bears with no ears

Each bear needs _____ ears

_____ extra ears

Real Bears

In this section of the Bears Unit students will learn about the North American bears—grizzly, black, polar, and Alaskan brown. The emphasis will be on facts in contrast to the stories of the first part of the unit. A goal is for students to learn to distinguish between fiction and nonfiction.

Many of the activities in this section will need to be done as a group so the teacher can help with the reading. A suggested plan for using the pages appears below, but should be adapted to fit our classroom.

Teacher Preparations:

- Use page 42 to make a bear facts list for display. Leave room to add more facts.
- Enlarge chart (page 43) to be filled in as information is gained. Pictures for chart are on page 44.
- Use page 54 as a reference to locate the ranges of the various bears on a wall map.

Sample Plan

Day 1

- Read, discuss, and color "Grizzly Bears" fact sheet (page 45)
- Share other materials about grizzlies
- Fill in Comparing Real Bears chart about grizzlies
- Use the map to locate where grizzly bears live (see page 54)
- Do "Grizzly Paws" worksheet (page 46)
- Have students write and/or draw about grizzlies

Day 2

- Read, discuss, and color "Black Bears" fact sheet (page 47)
- Share other materials about black bears Fill in Comparing Real Bears chart about black bears
- Use the map to locate where black bears live (see page 54)
- Do "Spring Summer Fall Winter" worksheet (page 48)
- Have students write and/or draw about black bears

Day 3

- Read, discuss, and color "Polar Bears" fact sheet (page 49)
- Share other materials about polar bears

- Fill in Comparing Real Bears chart about polar bears
- Use the map to locate where polar bears live (see page 54)
- Do "Bear Tracks" worksheet (page 50). Use fact sheets to help
- Have students write and/or draw about polar bears

Day 4

- Read, discuss, and color "Alaskan Brown Bears" fact sheet (page 51)
- Share other materials about brown bears
- Fill in the Comparing Real Bears chart about brown bears
- Use the map to locate where brown bears live (see page 54)
- Do "Which Bear Am I?" worksheet (page 52)
- Have students write and/or draw about brown bears

Day 5

- Read, discuss, and color "Did You Know...?" worksheet (page 53)
- Assemble bear work into a booklet
- Use "Share the Forest" worksheet (page 55); students should choose and complete one or more activities

All About Bears

1. There are 7 kinds of bears in the world.

2. Bears are big.

3. Bears walk flat-footed like people.

4. Bears can hear and smell well.

5. Bears will eat almost anything.

6. Most bears sleep all winter.

7. Most bears live in the forest.

8. Bears are mammals. They have fur. They feed their babies milk from their bodies. They take care of their babies for a long time.

42

Comparing Real Bears

	Grizzly Bears	Black Bears	Polar Bears	Brown Bear
Where do they live?				
What color are they?				
How long do cubs stay with their mom?				
What do they eat?				
Where do they make their den?				

Directions: Enlarge this chart using the pictures on page 44. Fill in as a group. The categories may be changed if you wish.

Real Bear Pictures

Suggested Use: Make a large chart like the one on page 43 to be filled in by the class while studying real bears.

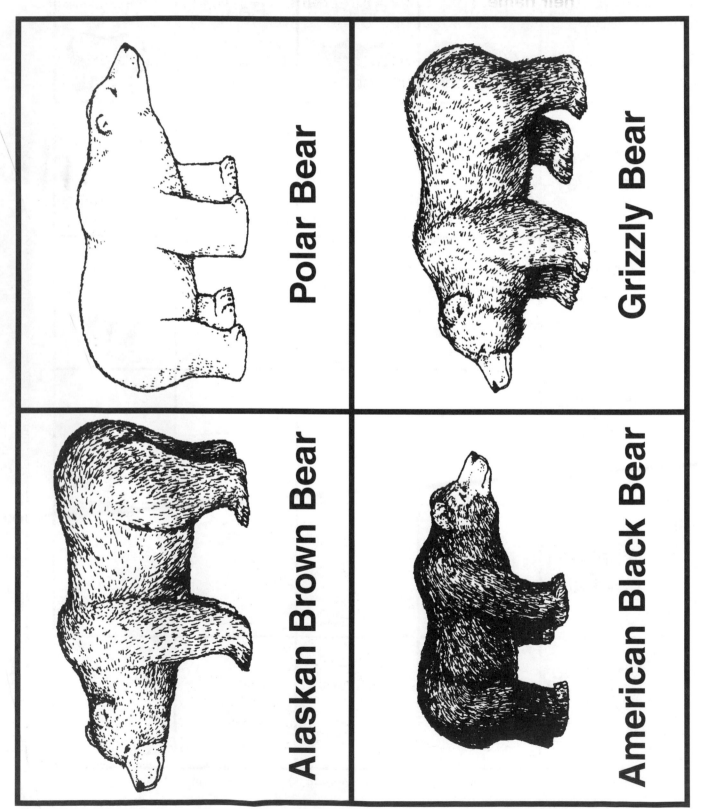

Grizzly Bears

Grizzly bears live In the Rocky Mountains, Alaska, and western Canada. They have brown fur with silver tips. This makes them look old or "grizzled." That's how they got their name. They have round ears, small eyes, a very short tail, and a hump on their shoulders. Their paws have long, sharp claws.

Grizzly bears eat lots of nuts, berries, and other food in the fall to get fat. They dig a den in the hillside under some tree roots. Then they sleep all winter and do not even eat.

Mother grizzlies have two or three cubs during the winter. The cubs nurse from their mother.

In the spring the bears come out of their dens. Mother grizzly teaches her cubs how to hunt for mice, beetles, roots, and other food. She teaches them how to be safe. The cubs may stay with their mother for two or three years. Father grizzly does not help with the cubs.

Grizzly Bears

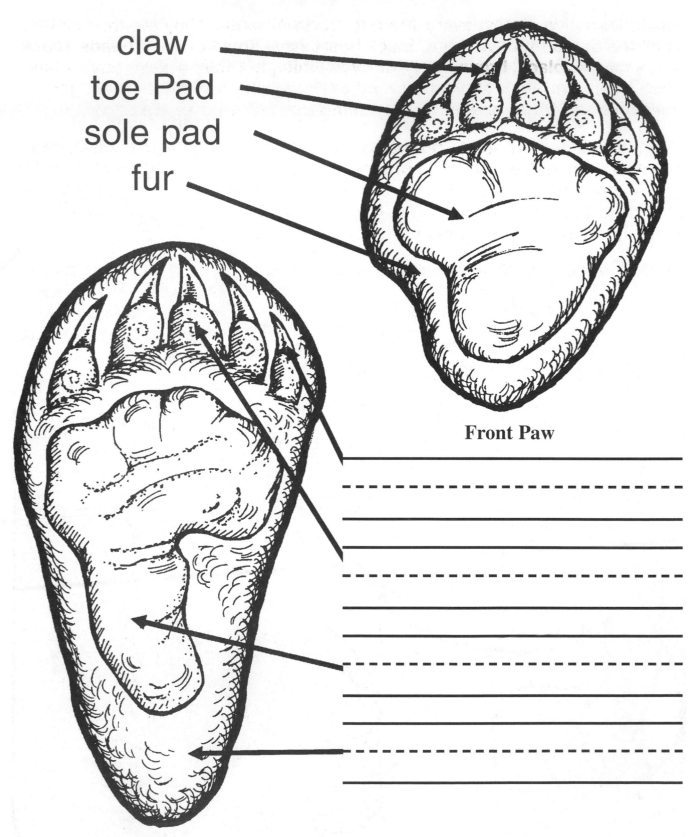

claw

toe Pad

sole pad

fur

Front Paw

Back Paw

Black Bears

Black bears live almost everywhere in North America. They are the smallest of all the bears that live there. Black bears have small pointed heads. Black bears can be black, brown, gray, or even white; but they always have a tan nose. Their claws are shorter than other bears and that makes them good tree climbers. Other bears can only climb trees when they are cubs.

One favorite den for spending the winter is a hollow log. Mother black bear has new cubs in January or February. The cubs will be with their mother for one and one-half years until they can take care of themselves. Father black bear does not help with the cubs. Mother black bear teaches her cubs to swim, hunt, and how to climb trees for safety.

Black bears eat the bulbs of violets and lilies, wild onions, honey, grubs and ants. They also like to dig for mice and moles. In late summer they hunt for all kinds of wild berries to eat.

Spring Summer Fall Winter

Write the season.

_____
- - - - - - - - - - - - - - - - - - -
_____

Bears come out of their dens.

_____
- - - - - - - - - - - - - - - - - - -
_____

Mother bears teach their cubs
to find food and be safe.

_____
- - - - - - - - - - - - - - - - - - -
_____

Bears eat a lot to get fat.

_____
- - - - - - - - - - - - - - - - - - -
_____

Bears sleep in their dens.

Polar Bears

Polar bears live near the North Pole. Polar Bears have yellow-white fur. They also have a black nose, small eyes and black lips. They have a long neck and a small narrow head. They have thick fur covering their feet so they can walk on ice.

Most polar bears do not sleep all winter. They stay out and hunt. They are meat-eaters. They hunt seals, walruses, and birds.

When she Is ready to have cubs, a mother polar bear goes Inland and digs a hole in the snow and then lets new snow cover her. Her warm breath keeps a little hole open In the snow. When her cubs are born, they have very little fur and pink skin.

Baby polar bear cubs stay with their mother for almost two years. She teaches them how to hunt and swim. Mother polar bear Is very strong and often carries or swims with her cubs on her back. Father polar bear does not help with the cubs.

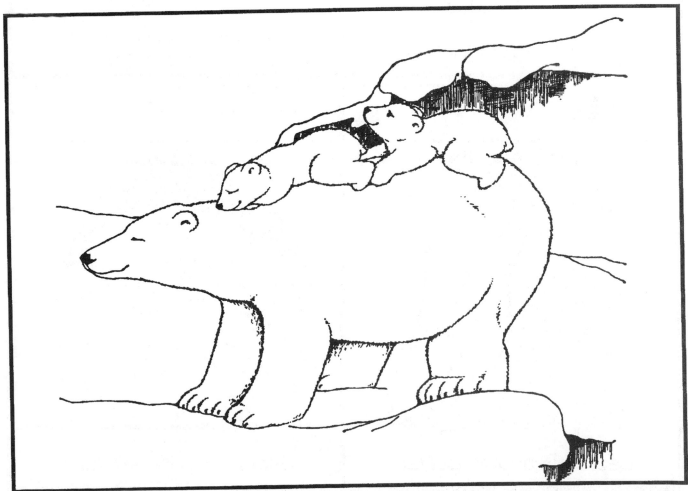

Bear Tracks

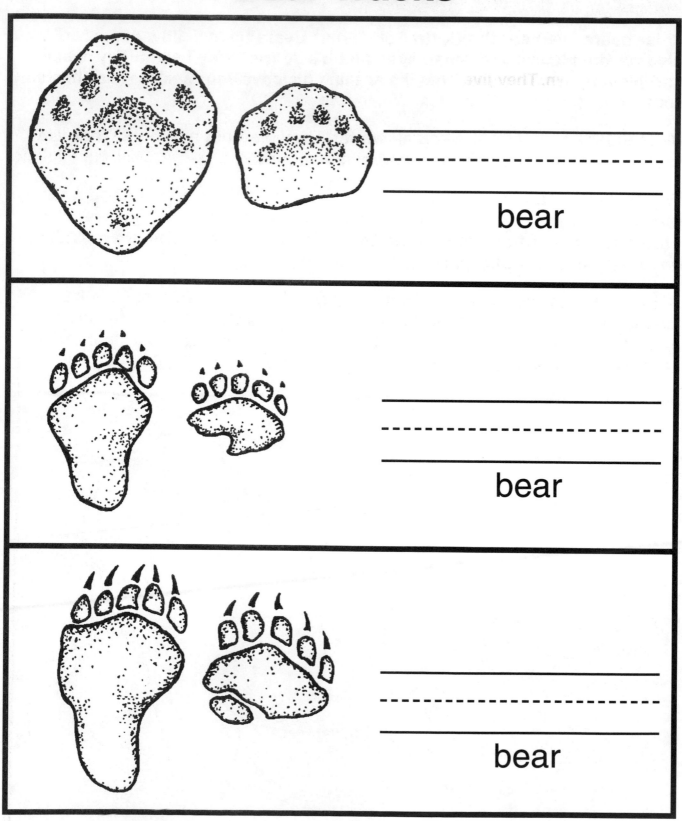

_____
- - - - - - - - - - - - - - - - - -
_____
bear

_____
- - - - - - - - - - - - - - - - - -
_____
bear

_____
- - - - - - - - - - - - - - - - - -
_____
bear

grizzly   black   polar

Name_____   *Science*

Alaskan Brown Bears

Alaskan Brown Bears are very big and look a lot like teddy bears. They are all shades of brown. They live near the sea and on islands in Alaska. These bears are also known as the Great Fisherman Bears.

Alaskan Brown Bears eat grass, cabbage roots, and other plants, but they like salmon the best. They use their curved claws for fishing. Brown bear cubs follow their mother to the Bering Sea to find salmon.

In November, when it gets cold, the bear family returns to Its den in the rocky cliff. They sleep there for the winter. By the time the cubs are about one and a half years old they can take care of themselves.

Which Bear Am I?

1. I live near the North Pole. _____ -------------------- **bear** _____	2. I am good at fishing. _____ -------------------- **bear** _____
3. I am the smallest North American bear. _____ -------------------- **bear** _____	4. I live in the Rocky Mountains. _____ -------------------- **bear** _____
5. I am a good tree climber. _____ -------------------- **bear** _____	6. I have a hump on my shoulders. _____ -------------------- **bear** _____
7. I live in Alaska where I can catch salmon. _____ -------------------- **bear** _____	8. My fur is yellow–white to help me hide. _____ -------------------- **bear** _____

Grizzly Bear

Black Bear

Polar Bear

Brown Bear

Did You Know...?

Koalas and pandas are not really members of the bear family.

Some people call koalas bears because they look like teddy bears, They are not bears, They have a pouch for their babies, The koala's hands and feet look more like fingers than paws, Koalas eat the leaves from the eucalyptus trees found in Australia where they live.

Most scientists think that giant pandas are really more like raccoons than bears, These pandas live in the mountains of China. They eat a special kind of bamboo that grows there.

Bears of North America

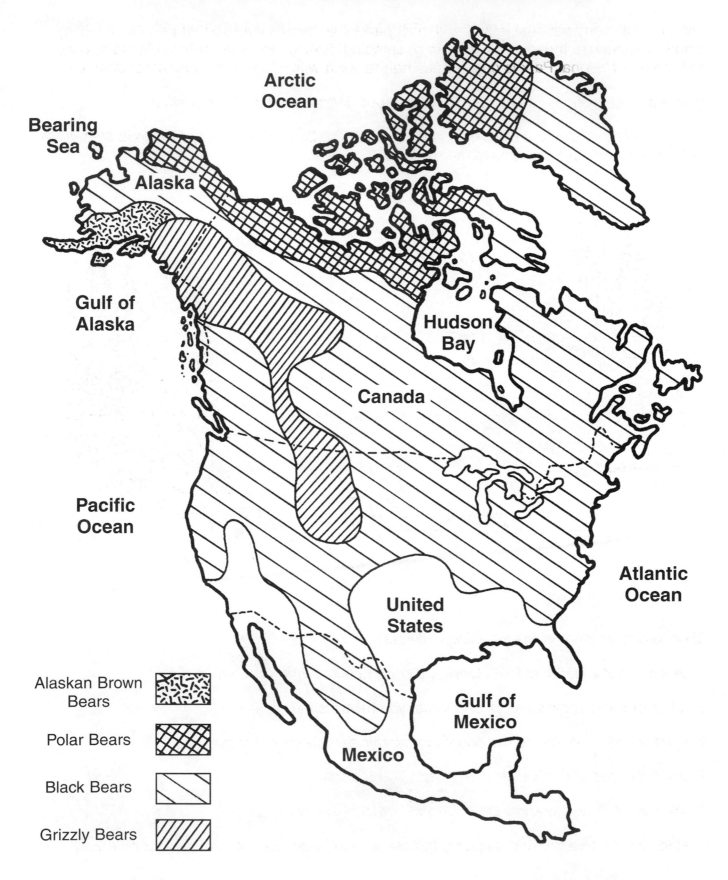

Arctic
Ocean

Bearing
Sea

Alaska

Gulf of
Alaska

Hudson
Bay

Canada

Pacific
Ocean

Atlantic
Ocean

United
States

Alaskan Brown
Bears

Gulf of
Mexico

Polar Bears

Mexico

Black Bears

Grizzly Bears

Share the Forest

The land for many national, state, and local parks has been saved so that people can enjoy nature. People use these areas for hiking, camping, fishing, and seeing animals in the wild. Yellowstone National Park is one famous natural area with many bears and other animals.

Wild animals, including bears, can be dangerous. People should not feed them.

The forest should be kept clean and safe. Smokey the Bear and Woodsy Owl were created to remind people about manners in the woods.

Choose one or more of the following activities:

1. Learn about a National Park. Draw a picture to share when you tell about it.

2. Tell about and show pictures of a forest you have visited.

3. Make a poster to remind the people to be safe and clean in the forest.

4. Draw pictures of animals you might see in the woods.

5. Make a list of health and safety rules for a trip to the forest.

6. Plan and go on a pretend camping trip. Be sure to follow good health and safety rules.

Drawing Bears

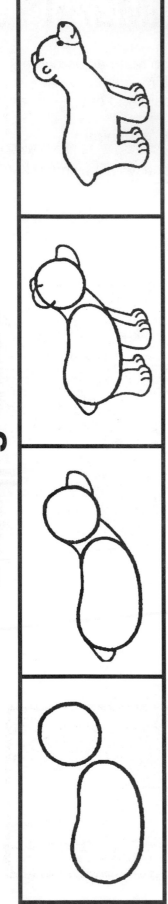

Follow the steps to draw your own bears. Practice on another piece of paper. Then make a bear scene below. Include at least one bear cub, a tree, some logs and some background. Use your crayons to add color.

"Bears in the Forest" Mural

Children enjoy constructing class murals, and with a little help from the teacher, everyone can participate in a successful project.

1. Hang butcher paper (children's height) in a good working location.

2. With the class, decide what the woods or forest would look like during the season or season(s) they will depict in the mural; i.e., ground, trees, bushes, other animals. List these for the students' reference.

3. Remind the students of the different "homes" in which bears might spend their winter.

4. Talk about and show some artwork by famous artists where animals are in their natural surroundings (e.g., John James Audubon, *Birds of America*).

   Point out:
   - Background and foreground
   - Size of objects in each part
   - Color variety/repetition
   - Use whole area

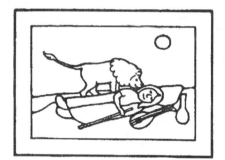

5. Decide on medium(s) to use for mural.

   Hint: Paint tree trunks and then sponge paint leaves for an easy way to complete background and use whole area.

6. Decide how to divide up the rest of the project.

   Hint: It often works well for small groups to work on the mural for a limited time once "the plan" is made. Or, to ensure participation by everyone, divide students into groups to make and color their own pieces to be glued onto the class mural background.

Bear Patterns

See Art Center, page 8, for suggested uses.

Berry Delightful Music

There are many cute songs about bears. Have children bring appropriate records, tapes, and videos to share.

Winnie-the-Pooh

After reading some or all of the stories in A.A. Milne's *Winnie-the-Pooh* and *The House at Pooh Corner,* watch some of the Disney short films or videos depicting Pooh Bear and company. Learn the songs from the film using a Disney record or tape for help.

The Bear Went Over the Mountain

The classic silly song, "The Bear Went Over the Mountain," can be used to reinforce that the grizzly bear lives in or near the Rocky Mountains. The words may be modified to teach the habitats of other bears.

	Original	**Sample Variation**
Verse 1:	The bear went over the mountain. The bear went over the mountain. The bear went over the mountain. To see what he could see.	The polar bear went out on an ice floe, The polar bear went out on an ice floe, The polar bear went out on an ice floe, To see what he could see.
Verse 2:	The other side of the mountain, The other side of the mountain, The other side of the mountain, Was all that he could see.	The frozen Arctic Ocean, The frozen Arctic Ocean, The frozen Arctic Ocean, Was all that he could see.

Hint: Substitute "grizzly" for bear.

Wee Sing Song Books and Tapes

Pam Beall and Susan Nipp have a series of children's song books and tapes. *Wee Sing Fun 'n Folk* tape and song book set (Price, Stern, and Sloan, 1989) has "The Bear" and "Grizzly Bear" among its many fun tunes.

Teddy Bear's Picnic

The delightful children's song is a must for use at the unit culmination party (see page 62). Green Tiger Press (1983) publishes an illustrated book, "Teddy Bear's Picnic" by Jimmy Kennedy, with a record of the song included.

Bear Treats

Bear Porridge

Equipment: Electric fry pan with cover; measuring cups and spoons; stirring spoon; small plastic cups and spoons for dishes.

Ingredients: 4 cups (1L) water, ³/₄ tsp. (4 mL) salt, 2 cups (500 mL) quick oats, raisins, cinnamon, sugar (brown and white), milk

Directions:

- Bring water to a boil.
- Add oats and salt.
- Cook 5 minutes or longer, stirring constantly.
- Turn off heat.
- Cover and let stand a few minutes. (Take a walk "in the woods" while the porridge is cooling.)
- Let students add raisins, cinnamon, sugar and milk as desired.

Bear Sugar Cookies

These simple sugar cookies require an oven at school. If no oven is available, use the No-Bake Chocolate Oatmeal Cookies below.

Use prepared sugar cookie dough. Follow directions for rolling out dough. Let students cut out their own bears with a bear cookie cutter (available in most houseware departments). Let the students decorate their own cookies with raisins, sprinkles, chocolate chips, etc. Bake according to directions and enjoy with milk or punch after lunch.

No-Bake Chocolate Oatmeal Cookies

Mix:
2 cups (500 mL) sugar
½ cup (125 mL) butter or margarine
½ cup (125 mL) canned milk
Boil 3 minutes stirring constantly.
Remove from heat.

Add:
1 cup (250 mL) small marshmallows
½ cup (125 mL) sifted cocoa powder
3 cups (750 mL) quick oats

Drop at once on wax paper. Work fast while the mixture is hot; it hardens quickly as it cools.

Makes about 3 dozen.

60

Beary Fun Games

Bear Bag Toss

Cut holes from a large cardboard bear or bear head (you may enlarge one of the patterns on page 58) for a bean bag toss. Assign points to each hole. Hang between two chairs. Students take turns tossing small bean bags at the target. An adult or upper grade student may keep score.

Nuts and Berries Hunt

Cardboard nuts and berries (patterns, page 77) with points printed on them are hidden around the room (or outdoor area). Students "hunt in the woods" for food. They total their score with the help of someone older, if necessary.

Spring Bears–Winter Bears

Adapt the children's game "Red Light-Green Light." When the leader calls, "Spring Bears," the players may move forward, but must stop to sleep when the leader calls, "Winter Bears."

Bears in the Den

Adapt the children's game "Squirrel in the Tree." Divide the class into groups of three. Two children join hands to form a "den." A third child is the "bear" inside the "den." There should be one or two extra children. When the leader shouts, "Spring," the bears leave their dens and join the extra children to run around the playing area. If "summer" or "fall" is called, the bears continue to run around outside the dens. When "winter" is called, each bear must leave the game. A new round begins with one of the den groups becoming the extra children.

Bear Walk

On all fours, students practice walking like bears: right hand, left foot—left hand, right foot. Chant the pattern aloud, slowly at first and then a little faster. This is good practice for right-left recognition.

Teddy Bears' Picnic

Students need an opportunity to celebrate and share what they have learned and experienced as part of their Bear Unit. A great way for them to do this is to invite guests to their classroom for a "Teddy Bears' Picnic." Keep in mind that a picnic does not need to take place outside, nor does it need to be a whole meal. Sharing a snack with other children or adults is very rewarding to students. It will also give them an opportunity to serve as hosts, practice manners, write invitations (see page 63), decorate, entertain, and share their stories, books and other completed activities with an audience.

Use the ideas below only as a guide. Students really need to work in teams or as a class to plan and prepare for their own Teddy Bears' Picnic.

- Have the students prepare a snack for their picnic. Possible treats might include peanut butter and honey sandwiches, berry juice, mixed nuts, fresh fruit, oatmeal cookies, or prepare one of the recipes on page 60.

- Students take guests on a tour of the classroom. The students should explain all bear work including team and class activities.

- Students read stories they have written, with or to guests.

- Students use stick puppets to retell *Goldilocks and the Three Bears.*

- Students use panel stories to retell *Good As New.*

- Students give reports on the four nonfiction bears.

- Students participate in a program for guests, including poetry, songs and games. (see pages 29, 59, and 61)

- Guests bring a favorite bear to share with the students.

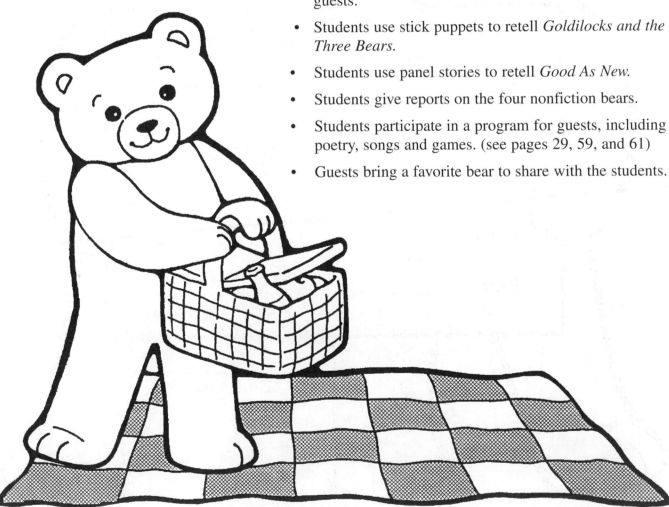

Invitation

1. Color the bears
2. Fill in invitation.
3. Cut out.
4. Fold on center line.

Please bring your favorite teddy bear and come to our Teddy Bears' Picnic.

Date:_____

Time:_____

Place: _____

From: _____

The Bears' Picnic Gameboard

Color gameboard and glue inside file folder.

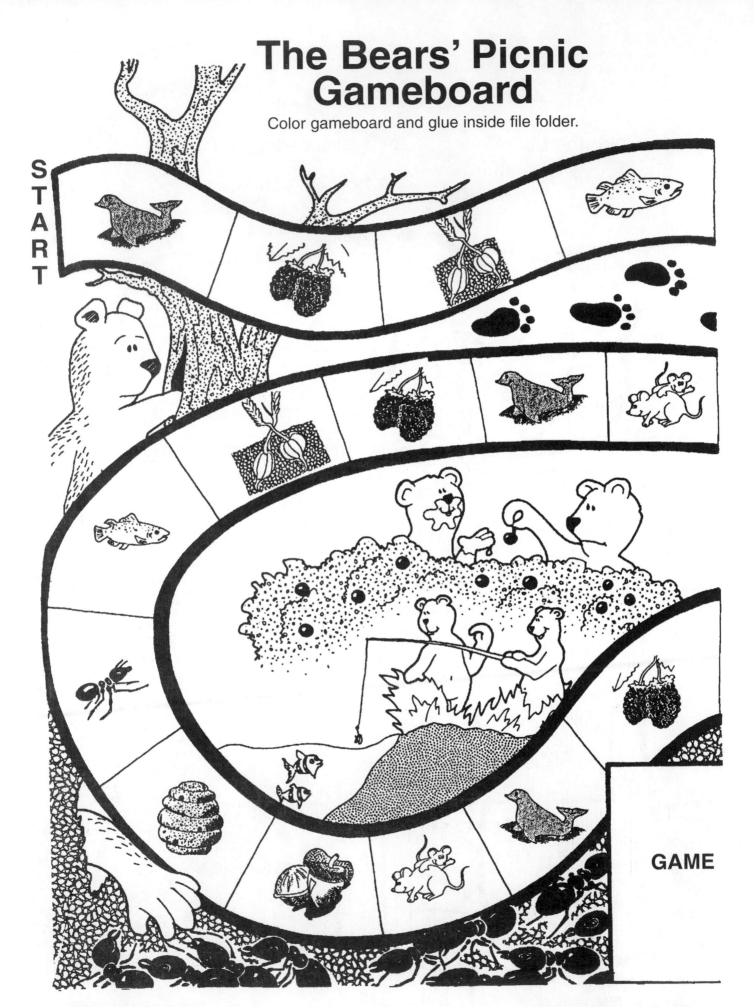

START

GAME

64

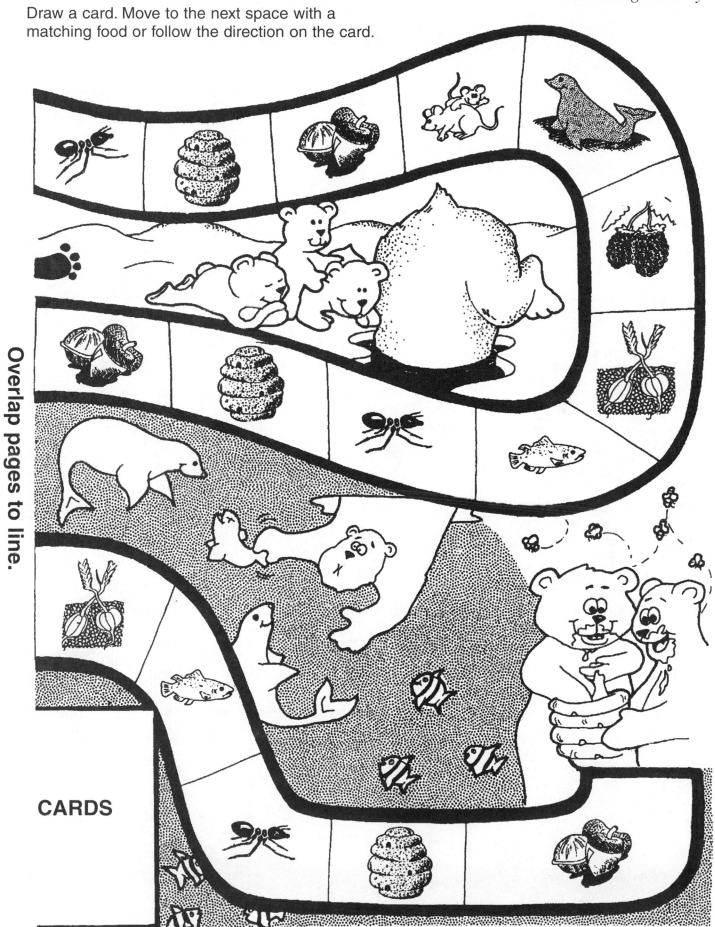

Draw a card. Move to the next space with a matching food or follow the direction on the card.

Overlap pages to line.

CARDS

Gameboard Cards

Duplicate four of each on heavy paper.

Color, cut out, and laminate.

Use with gameboard (pages 64 and 65).

Find good food.

Move 2 spaces.

Sleep all winter.

Lose a turn.

Beary Good Bulletin Board

Objective

This bulletin board may be used to call children's attention to materials of the teacher's choice. (See Suggested Uses below.)

Materials

Background paper; construction paper; scissors; stapler; pushpins; materials to be displayed; patterns from pages 68-70

Construction

Reproduce patterns onto appropriately colored construction paper and cut out.

Make banner for bears to hold, inserting the name of the materials you are displaying. (See Suggested Uses below.)

Attach background paper. Assemble all pieces as shown above; attach with staples or pushpins.

Suggested Uses

Use the bulletin board to display:
- Children's work (Beary Good Work)
- Children's writing (Beary Good Writing)
- Children's artwork (Beary Good Art)
- A collection of bear photographs (Beary Good Pictures)

- Book covers to encourage reading (Beary Good Books)
- Vocabulary lists from the bear unit (Beary Good Words)
- Facts about real bears (Beary Good Things to Know)

Make the bulletin board interactive by having the bears hold problems or questions. Supply a container of answer cards. have children match answers to problem by slipping the cards under the correct bears' feet.

Patterns

See
suggested
uses, page
67.

arm

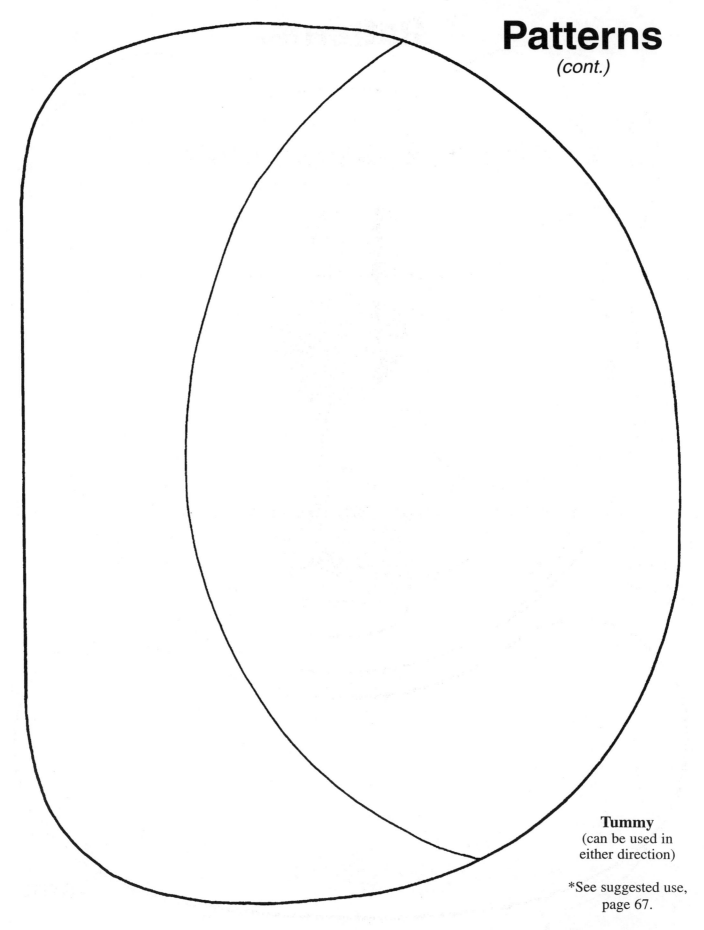

Tummy
(can be used in
either direction)

*See suggested use,
page 67.

Patterns (cont.)

leg

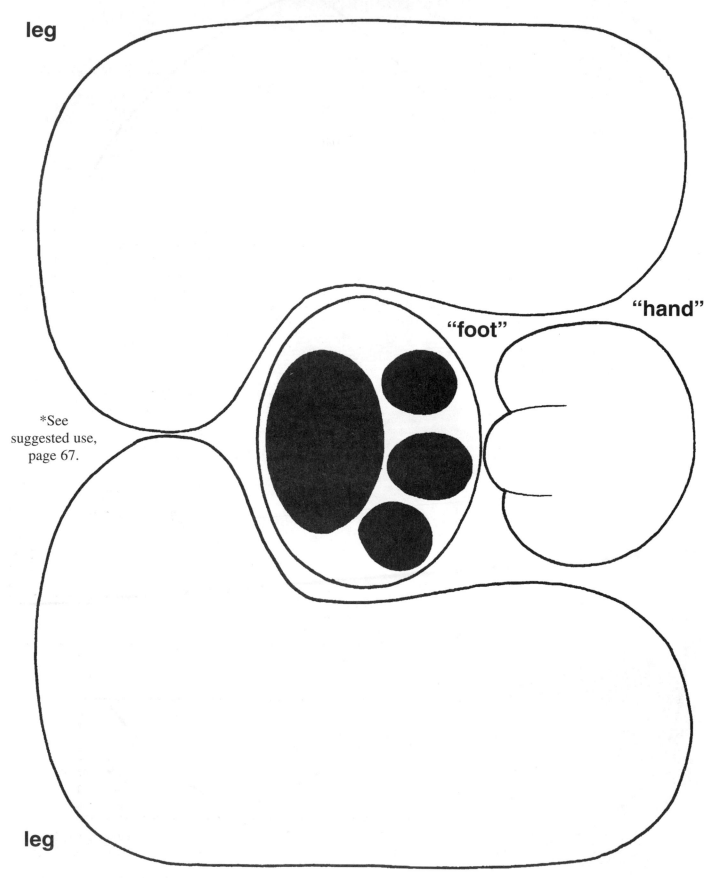

"foot"

"hand"

*See
suggested use,
page 67.

leg

Patterns

Bear Badge *(See page 7)*

If you have a badge maker, use this pattern to make a bear button for your students.

Or, mount it on tagboard with a safety pin taped to the back.

Reading Coupons *(See page 9)*

Beary Good
Reading Today!

Beary Good
Reading Today!

Beary Good
Reading Today!

Reading Tickets *(See page 22)*

I read my panel story to…
_____

I read my panel story to…
_____

I read my panel story to…
_____

Bookmark *(See page 23)*

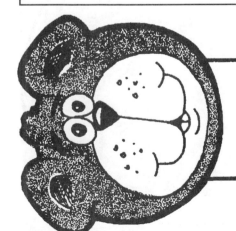

It's beary fun to read!

Name ____

Awards

Congratulations!

_____

*did a beary good job
on the Famous Bear Unit.*

_____   _____

teacher   date

This
"Beary Wonderful Award"

is given to _____
for being a great cooperative worker during our
Famous Bear Unit.

_____

teacher

_____

date

Bear Record Form

Name																
1.																
2.																
3.																
4.																
5.																
6.																
7.																
8.																
9.																
10.																
11.																
12.																
13.																
14.																
15.																
16.																
17.																
18.																
19.																
20.																
21.																
22.																
23.																
24.																
25.																
26.																
27.																
28.																
29.																
30.																

Visiting Bear

Dear Parents,

Tonight is your child's turn to have our class bear spend the night. Your child may dress the bear or add to his or her special suitcase. Please help your child make a picture postcard for the class.

Be sure that your child returns the bear, the suitcase, and completed postcard on the next school day, because other children are waiting for their turn to have the bear spend the night.

The bear is your child's responsibility, but your help is greatly appreciated.

Sincerely,

_____ **and room** _____

Postcard From Home…

When it's your turn to take our class bear to visit your house, you will need to "send" the class a postcard. Write a note, address the postcard to our class at school, and draw a picture about your family and the bear on the front.

Letters Home

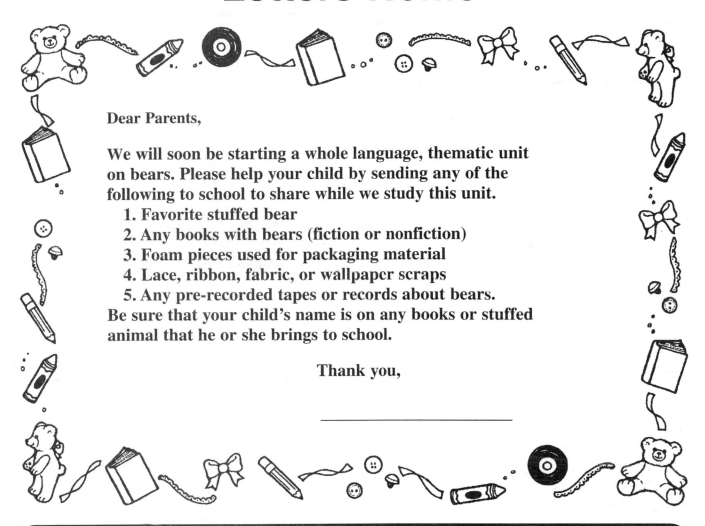

Dear Parents,

We will soon be starting a whole language, thematic unit on bears. Please help your child by sending any of the following to school to share while we study this unit.
   1. Favorite stuffed bear
   2. Any books with bears (fiction or nonfiction)
   3. Foam pieces used for packaging material
   4. Lace, ribbon, fabric, or wallpaper scraps
   5. Any pre-recorded tapes or records about bears.
Be sure that your child's name is on any books or stuffed animal that he or she brings to school.

   Thank you,

   _____

Dear Parents,

Can you help with our cooking project?

If so, please send _____
                                (ingredients)

on or before _____.
                                (date)

Thank you,

Bear Hungry Room_____

P.S. If you are available to help the class cook on

_____at _____,
        (date)   (time)

please send a note to_____.
                                (teacher)

Hear Me—See Me

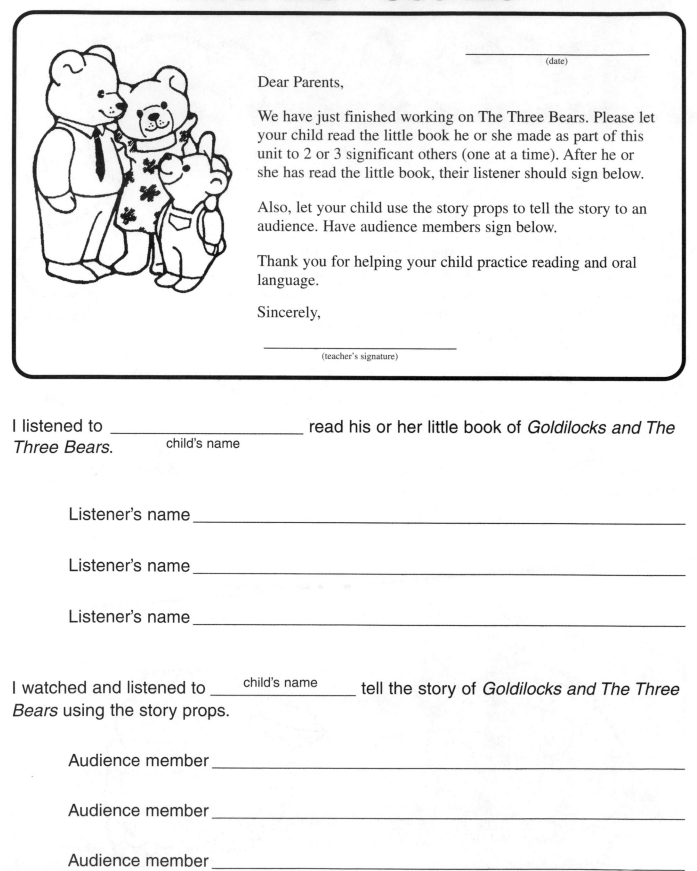

_____
(date)

Dear Parents,

We have just finished working on The Three Bears. Please let your child read the little book he or she made as part of this unit to 2 or 3 significant others (one at a time). After he or she has read the little book, their listener should sign below.

Also, let your child use the story props to tell the story to an audience. Have audience members sign below.

Thank you for helping your child practice reading and oral language.

Sincerely,

_____
(teacher's signature)

I listened to _____ read his or her little book of *Goldilocks and The Three Bears*.
child's name

Listener's name _____

Listener's name _____

Listener's name _____

I watched and listened to _____child's name_____ tell the story of *Goldilocks and The Three Bears* using the story props.

Audience member _____

Audience member _____

Audience member _____

76

Little Bear Patterns

Kind of Bears:_____

Fact: _____

_____

_____

Title:_____

_____

_____

Author: _____

_____

Bear Facts: As students learn about real bears, they may write or dictate a fact to be posted on a chart or bulletin board near the science center. See page 8.

Reading Bears: Students try to see how many books about bears they can find and read. As they share a book with the class, they fill out and post a bear on a Beary Good Books chart or bulletin board.

Game Pieces

*Use with "Nuts and Berries Hunt," (page 61)

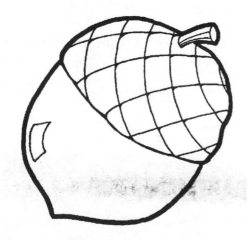

78

Bibliography

Core Books

Douglass, Barbara. *Good as New.* Mulberry, 1982.
Eisen, Arnold (retold by). *Goldilocks and the Three Bears.* Knopf, 1989.

Other Versions of *Goldilocks*

Cauley, Lorinda Bryan (retold by). *Goldilocks and the Three Bears.* Putnam, 1981.
Galdone, Paul (retold by). *The Three Bears.* Houghton Mifflin, 1979.
Laird, Donivee Martin. *Will Wai Kula and the Three Mongooses.* Barnaby, 1983. (Hawaiian version)
Marshall, James (retold by). *Goldilocks and the Three Bears.* Dial, 1988.
Turkle, Brinton. *Deep in the Forest.* Dutton, 1987. (a reverse Goldilocks)
Yolen, Jane. *The Three Bears Rhyme Book.* HBJ, 1987.

Fiction

Alexander, Martha. *Blackwood Bear.* Dial, 1976.
Asch, Frank. *Happy Birthday Moon.* Prentice-Hall, 1982, and other books by Asch.
Berenstain, Stan and Jan. *The Berenstain Bears series.* Random House.
Doerksen, Nan. *Bears for Breakfast.* Kindred, 1983.
Freeman, Don. *Corduroy and A Pocket for Corduroy.* Penguin, 1968, 1978.
Hoban, Lillian. *Arthur's Honey Bear.* Harper & Row, 1974.
Martin, Bill Jr. *Brown Bear, Brown Bear, What Do You See?* Holt, 1970.
McCloskey, Robert. *Blueberries for Sal.* Puffin, 1987.
Milne, A.A. *Winnie-the-Pooh* and *The House at Pooh Corner.* Dell, 1970.
Minarik, Elsie H. *Little Bear series.* Hasper.
Peet, Bill. *Big Bad Bruce.* Houghton Mifflin, 1977.
Rosen, Michael. *We're Going on a Bear Hunt.* Macmillan, 1989.
Waber, Bernard. *Ira Sleeps Over.* Scholastic, 1972.
Ward, Lynd. *The Biggest Bear.* Houghton Mifflin, 1952.

Nonfiction

AIMS Education Foundation. "Friendly Bears" manipulative counters and *Primarily Bears.*
   P.O. Box 8120, Fresno, CA 93747. (209) 255-4094
Freschet, Bernice. *Grizzly Bear.* Scribner, 1975.
Graham, Ada and Frank. *Bears in the Wild.* Delacorte, 1981.
Hennefrund, Bet. *What Makes a Mammal?* Mulberry, 1982.
Johnson, Ginny and Judy Cutchins. *Andy Bear.* Scholastic, 1985.
Leach, Michael. *Bears.* Mallard, 1990.
Nentl, Jerolyn. *The Grizzly.* Crestwood House, Mankato, MN 1984.
Patent, Dorothy H. *Bears of the Wild.* Holiday House, 1980.
Steiner, Barbara. *Biographies of a Polar Bear.* Putnam, 1972.
Van Wormer, Joe. *The World of the Black Bear.* Lippincott, 1966.

Music

Kennedy, Jimmy. *Teddy Bears' Picnic.* Green Tiger Press, 1983. (book and record)
Glaser, Tom (Compiled by). *Treasury of Songs for Children.* Doubleday, 1964. "The Bear Went Over the Mountain."

Answer Key

p. 16

Goldilocks	hot	cottage
cold	right	hard
bears	soft	home

p. 33

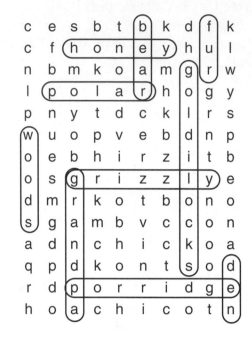

p. 34

bear	bare	bear
bare	bear	bear

p. 36

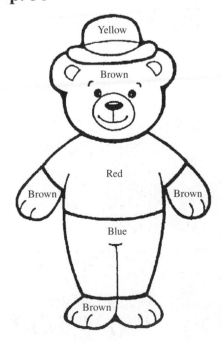

p. 39

3 Children	4 swings
1 swing left over	
2 children	3 wagons
1 wagon left over	
4 children	2 bears
2 children with no bear	

p. 40

4 needles	2 spools of thread
2 extra needles	
2 children	2 boxes of popcorn
0 extra popcorn	
7 ears	2 bears with no ears
Each bear needs 2 ears	
3 extra ears.	

p. 50

polar
black
grizzly

p. 52

1. polar

2. brown

3. black

4. grizzly

5. black

6. grizzly

7. brown

8. polar